A Chef's Laboratory

Written by Susan Griffiths

Contents	Page
Chapter 1. *A Kitchen Laboratory*	4
Chapter 2. *Common Chemical Changes*	7
Chapter 3. *Scientific Sweets!*	14
Chapter 4. *Lip-Smacking Lab Recipes*	20
Chapter 5. *Lovely Laboratory Loaf*	26
Index And Bookweb Links	32
Glossary	Inside Back Cover

Chapter Snapshots

1. A Kitchen Laboratory
Page 4

In many ways, a kitchen is like a laboratory. A chef uses kitchen equipment to change the way that foods look, smell and taste. But what they're really doing is changing the chemicals in the food!

2. Common Chemical Changes   Page 7

To understand what happens when a chef works in a kitchen, we need to understand some common chemical changes. They're the same changes that occur in a laboratory — but much tastier!

"A kitchen is a lot like

3. Scientific Sweets!
Page 14

Now comes the fun part, where we can use our scientific knowledge in a practical way. Follow the instructions for some delicious results.

4. Lip-Smacking Lab Recipes Page 20

If you want some mouth-watering smells and tastes to come from your kitchen laboratory, follow these simple experimental procedures!

5. Lovely Laboratory Loaf Page 26

Most people eat bread every day — but not everybody knows how to make their own delicious loaves. With a little work, time, and the right science knowledge, it's easy!

a science laboratory."

1. A Kitchen Laboratory

Ever since prehistoric times, people have been inventing new ways to make their food tasty and interesting. By experimenting with different foods, or ingredients, many attractive-tasting and nutritious dishes can be created in the kitchen.

A kitchen is a lot like a science laboratory. Instead of bunsen burners, beakers and test-tubes, it has a stove, ovens, pots and pans.

And a cook, or chef, is a lot like a scientist. A chef has studied how different chemicals change the ingredients in recipes during preparation and cooking.

In the following pages, find out how chefs use the equipment in their kitchen laboratories and combinations of ingredients to create a variety of chemical changes. But, unlike the chemical changes you might observe in a science laboratory, the results will be a lot more interesting and tasty!

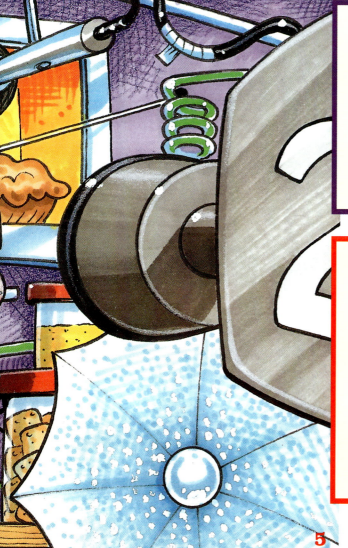

TV Chefs

Need ideas for cooking? Tune into a TV cooking segment. Many chefs present a wide variety of recipes on TV to inform and inspire people to cook *any* recipe from *any* country.

Why Do Onions Make Us Cry?

When we slice an onion, tiny droplets of the liquid inside onion cells can spray up into our eyes. As soon as this liquid starts to sting us, our eyes produce tears to help dilute and wash away the stinging liquid.

Safety First

Just like a science laboratory, the kitchen is a place where safety rules must always be followed!

1. Never cook in a kitchen without adult supervision.
2. Always take extra care with kitchen tools, such as knives and electrical appliances.
3. Always be very careful around hot surfaces, like those in ovens and on stoves.
4. Always take special care around hot or boiling liquids.
5. Keep the kitchen clean and tidy, so people do not slip or fall.

And remember: when you have finished cooking, your food may still be extremely hot. Let it cool down to a safe temperature before tasting!

Experienced chefs know how to safely cook foods using open flames — but they always take care not to burn themselves.

2. Common Chemical Changes

There are some common chemical changes that happen when we cook certain foods and drinks. It's important to know what some of these chemical changes are, and why they happen, before we start working with the recipes in the following chapters.

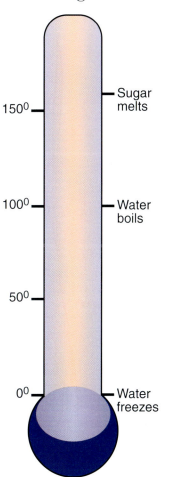

Melting And Hardening

When you put water into a freezer, and the temperature drops below zero degrees celsius, it turns from a liquid into a solid block of ice! If you heat the block of ice above zero degrees again, it melts and returns to a liquid.

Many other substances can also melt or solidify at different temperatures. Sugar melts at a temperature of 160^0 C. At temperatures below 160^0 C, it 'freezes' and becomes a solid again. Butter melts at 20^0 C. Salt melts at 801^0 C!

Celsius

The abbreviation for Celsius is 'C'. Example: 100^0 C = one hundred degrees Celsius. Celsius is a metric measure of temperature based on the freezing and boiling point of water — 0^0 C for freezing, 100^0 C for boiling. This scale was devised by a Swedish astronomer, Anders Celsius, in 1742.

Cooks often cook with oils and fats. Oils, such as olive oil, are liquid. Fats, such as butter, are a solid, because they only change into a liquid state at about 20^0 C. By reducing the melted butter's temperature, it hardens to a solid again.

Melting and hardening are two very important processes in cooking.

Boiling

Why are boiled potatoes softer than raw potatoes?

When water is heated to a temperature of 100^0 C, it starts to boil. Bubbles of steam appear, as the water turns from a liquid into a gas.

Boiling Points

Not all liquids boil at 100^0 C. Some, like alcohol, boil at the lower temperature of 78.5^0 C. Others, like vinegar, boil at the higher temperature of 118^0 C.

Cooks use heat from boiling liquids or from steam to cook foods. At 100^0 C, this heat breaks down the cells of things that were once living, such as vegetables (plants) or meats and fish (animals). This happens because cells are also full of water. When the water inside the cells boils, it bursts the walls of the cells. As cell walls break down and burst, food that was hard and tough becomes softer. This chemical change often makes the food tastier and easier for our bodies to digest.

Dissolving

When sugar or salt is placed into water, what happens?

When chemicals like salt and sugar are solid, their molecules are tightly joined together. But when these solid chemicals are mixed with water or other liquids, their molecules break apart, dissolve, and disappear into the liquid. Cooks dissolve a lot of chemicals in their cooking.

However, the molecular composition of many substances like flour, meat and vegetables means that they cannot dissolve in liquid.

What Is A Molecule?

A molecule is a group of atoms joined together to form a substance. Chemists use a special code to describe molecules. A water molecule has two hydrogen atoms and one oxygen atom, so its chemical code is H_2O. A sugar molecule has 12 carbon atoms, 22 hydrogen atoms and 11 oxygen atoms. Its code is $C_{12}H_{22}O_{11}$.

Sugar dissolves faster in warm water because the heat helps the molecules to break down.

Crystallisation

Once salt or sugar has dissolved in water, can it reappear?

Look at salt or sugar under a magnifying glass and you will see that it is made up of tiny, hard grains. These grains are called crystals. Although salt or sugar crystals easily dissolve in water, their molecules will join back together to form crystals again if we take away the water.

Water is easily 'taken away' by leaving it in the sun, or by boiling it until all the water has evaporated. The process of making crystals from a liquid is called crystallisation.

A Crystallisation Experiment

To show how crystallisation works, try the following experiment.

1. Fill a jar with water and dissolve five teaspoons of salt in it. Place a pencil over the jar with a piece of string sitting in the salty water.

2. 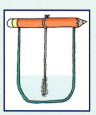 Place the jar in a warm place. After a few days, the water will start to evaporate and salt crystals will appear on the string.

3. Once all the water has evaporated, you should see a cluster of salt crystals on the string and at the bottom of the jar.

Mixing

When different ingredients are combined, the texture of the mixture may change. For example, flour and water mixed together form a thick paste, or dough. The dry flour doesn't dissolve — the water softens it to form a thick mixture.

Chemical Reactions

When two or more chemicals are mixed together, sometimes their molecules form a new, completely different chemical. When baking soda and water are mixed together, for example, a new chemical called carbon dioxide is formed. Carbon dioxide is a gas. This kind of change, where two chemicals have reacted to form a new chemical, is called a chemical reaction.

Carbon Monoxide

Carbon monoxide is a gas that is produced when we burn petrol inside motor vehicle engines. Although it is very similar to carbon dioxide, it is a deadly poison if we breathe too much of it. In most countries, there are laws to limit the amount of carbon monoxide a car engine can produce. These laws help to reduce the amount of pollution caused by the chemical reactions inside your car!

Heating

Why does toast burn and turn black when left in the toaster for too long?

Heating causes many chemical changes, apart from melting or boiling. All things that were once living, like many of our foods, contain chemicals called carbon, hydrogen and oxygen. If hydrogen and oxygen are heated for long enough, they will burn away. Only carbon, which is a brown or black chemical, will remain — just like a piece of toast left in a toaster for too long.

When we want foods to cook and turn a golden brown colour on the outside, we usually heat them in a frypan, in an oven, under a grill or over a flame. We can't boil them, because the water stops the oxygen and hydrogen from burning away!

Heating can also cause foods to dry out, as their water content usually evaporates. A cake baking in an oven changes from a runny, thick liquid mixture into a solid cake as the water evaporates and other chemical changes occur.

Protein Changing

Why do eggs turn hard when they are heated?

All living things contain chemicals called protein. Foods like meat, fish, eggs and milk all contain protein. These foods contain the protein that we can easily digest.

Protein behaves strangely when heated or mixed with other chemicals. Its molecules change shape. When they change shape, they can get so tangled up with each other that they can turn from a runny liquid into a solid. When an egg is boiled, the raw runny egg hardens because the heat tangles up all its protein molecules.

As you will see in Chapter 4, this is a very useful chemical process when we are working in our kitchen laboratory!

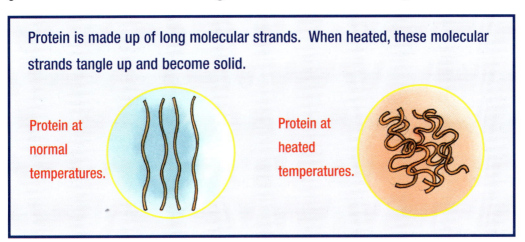

Protein is made up of long molecular strands. When heated, these molecular strands tangle up and become solid.

Protein at normal temperatures.

Protein at heated temperatures.

3. Scientific Sweets!

Something that can be eaten is called 'edible'. In these recipe experiments, chemicals or ingredients will be used to create two deliciously edible results: hokey pokey and rice pudding!

HOKEY POKEY

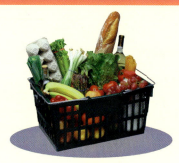

Chemicals you will need:

- 5 tablespoons of sugar.
- 2 tablespoons of golden syrup.
- 1 teaspoon of baking soda.

Equipment you will need:

- A stove.
- A small saucepan.
- A mixing spoon.
- A flat tin or tray that has been lightly greased with oil or butter.

REMEMBER: Read the safety rules on page 6 carefully before you begin this recipe experiment!

In this edible experiment, we want to first turn the sugar into a hot liquid. We can do this by heating it and dissolving it in another liquid, golden syrup. Golden syrup is a thick mixture of water and sugar.

DISSOLVING

Step 1: Heat the sugar and the golden syrup gently in a saucepan until the sugar dissolves.

BOILING

Step 2: Keep heating until the mixture starts to boil.

Step 3: Stir the mixture to prevent it burning. Then place the saucepan on a heat-resistant surface.

Now comes the fun part! We will now use a chemical called baking soda. When baking soda becomes wet and hot, a chemical reaction takes place. The baking soda gives off a gas called carbon dioxide, the same gas that makes soft-drinks fizzy.

> ### Diabetes
> Diabetes is an illness caused when the body is unable to break down or use sugar properly. Usually, an organ called the pancreas produces insulin, a chemical that controls the body's sugar levels. Diabetics need daily injections of insulin to help them control their sugar levels.

REACTING

Step 4: Stir the baking soda into the hot mixture quickly, until the mixture becomes frothy and bubbly.

Step 5: Quickly, but carefully, pour the frothy mixture into the greased tin.

CRYSTALLISATION

Step 6: Put in the fridge for 15 minutes until cold. As the sugary mixture cools down, it changes from a liquid into a solid again. The carbon dioxide bubbles are trapped inside the hard, sweet candy making it easier to crumble.

WHAT HAPPENED?

In your kitchen laboratory, several chemical reactions helped you to create a delicious sweet.

WHAT TO DO NOW?

All you have to do is break up your cooled hokey pokey and enjoy it! You can either eat it as candy, or you can crush it into smaller pieces and mix it through some ice-cream. If you do that, you'll have the perfect food to eat with your next edible experiment!

REACTING RICE PUDDING

Chemicals you will need:

- 5 tablespoons of short grain rice.
- 2 tablespoons of sugar.
- 2 cups of milk.
- 2–3 drops of vanilla essence.
- 1 teaspoon of butter or oil.
- 1/4 teaspoon of ground nutmeg.

Equipment you will need:

- An oven.
- An ovenproof dish.
- A mixing spoon.

REMEMBER: Read the safety rules on page 6 carefully before you begin this recipe experiment!

In this edible experiment, we need to turn rice from hard, inedible grains, into a soft, creamy pudding that will go perfectly with the hokey pokey ice-cream. By boiling the rice grains, their cell walls break down and soften. When starch (a chemical inside rice grains) is cooked, a chemical reaction makes each grain swell into larger, jelly-like grains four times their original size!

MIXING AND DISSOLVING

Step 1: Place the rice and the sugar in the ovenproof dish. Add milk and vanilla, mixing well.

Step 2: Add butter or oil. Sprinkle nutmeg over the top.

The sugar will dissolve in the milk and vanilla mixture. The other ingredients will also combine well during the baking process.

BOILING AND REACTING

Step 3: Bake in the oven at 150^0 C for two hours. In the first hour, carefully open the oven door once or twice to stir the mixture.

Ovens

Over 3,000 years ago, the Ancient Egyptians used simple ovens made out of clay to bake bread. The Romans, who lived 2,000 years ago, used ovens made out of stones, clay and tiles. Between 400–1800, most households cooked in pots over an open fire. Ovens were not common in most houses.

Wood-burning metal ovens were invented in 1800, and coal-burning ovens were invented in 1833. In 1860, gas became widely used for heating ovens. In the 1930s, electric ovens first became popular and, along with gas ovens, are still used today.

WHAT HAPPENED?

Where did all the milk go after it boiled? It was absorbed inside the grains of rice through the cell walls. The rice became soft. At the same time, the starch inside the rice reacted with the heat and moisture in the milk. The rice swelled, and became a solid pudding.

You may notice that the top of your rice pudding turned golden brown. This is because both rice and milk come from living things. A few of the hydrogen and oxygen molecules have burnt away in the oven, leaving a tasty layer of brown carbon.

WHAT TO DO NOW?

The experiment is over, and it's time to taste the results. Add fresh fruit and two scoops of hokey pokey ice-cream to your rice pudding, and enjoy!

4. Lip-Smacking Lab Recipes

In these lip-smacking recipe experiments, heat will tangle up some protein chemicals so much, the mixtures will turn from liquids into solids!

PROTEIN PIKELETS

Chemicals you will need:
- 1 cup of white flour.
- 1 teaspoon of baking soda.
- 1/4 teaspoon of salt.
- 1 egg.
- 1/4 cup of sugar.
- 3/4 cup of milk.
- A little butter.

Equipment you will need:
- A stove.
- A frypan or griddle.
- Two bowls.
- A mixing spoon.
- An eggbeater.

REMEMBER: Read the safety rules on page 6 carefully before you begin this recipe experiment!

In this experiment, the protein in the egg will turn the liquid mixture into solid pikelets. But another chemical reaction will ensure that the solid pikelets are light and fluffy.

MIXING

Step 1: In one bowl, mix the dry ingredients — flour, baking soda and salt.

DISSOLVING

Step 2: In the other bowl, beat the egg and the sugar together with the eggbeater, until the sugar dissolves and the mixture thickens.

MIXING

Step 3: Pour the egg and sugar mixture, together with the milk, into the bowl containing the dry ingredients. Mix with the mixing spoon until a smooth, thick liquid forms.

MELTING

Step 4: Put the butter into the preheated frypan and heat it on a medium heat setting until it melts.

PROTEIN CHANGING

Step 5: Drop spoonfuls of the thick liquid mixture into the frypan. The protein pikelet mix will spread out and start to turn into solid pikelets.

REACTING

Step 6: When bubbles appear on the top of each pikelet, turn them over. Cook your protein pikelets until they look golden on both sides.

WHAT HAPPENED?

The heat from the frypan and the hot butter tangled up the protein in the egg. The mixture turned from a liquid into solid pikelets.

At the same time, the heat and moisture reacted with the baking soda. Bubbles of carbon dioxide gas formed. Tear apart a protein pikelet, and you will see that it is filled with hundreds of tiny bubbles. It was this chemical reaction that made the solid pikelets light and fluffy.

The protein pikelets turned golden as tiny amounts of hydrogen and oxygen burnt away, leaving just the right amount of carbon on the outside of each pikelet.

WHAT TO DO NOW?

Your protein pikelets are ready to eat! Try them with jam, maple syrup, or some lemon juice and sugar. They're a particularly pleasant protein experiment!

CHEMICOOKIES

Chemicals you will need:

- 250 grams of soft butter.
- 1/2 cup of sugar.
- 1 teaspoon of vanilla essence.
- 1 egg.
- 3 cups of white flour.
- 2 tablespoons of cocoa.

Equipment you will need:

- An oven.
- A mixing spoon.
- A rolling pin.
- A knife or cookie cutter.
- An oven tray, lightly greased with some butter.

REMEMBER: Read the safety rules on page 6 carefully before you begin this recipe experiment!

If you prefer your cookies to be crunchy, make chemicookies. This recipe's mixture will use proteins to turn a liquid mixture into solid cookies. And, crystallisation will take place to add some crunch!

MELTING

Step 1: Put the butter in a warm place where it will soften — close to its melting point. It's soft texture will make it easy to use. But do not allow it to turn into liquid!

DISSOLVING

Step 2: Mix the soft butter, the sugar and the vanilla essence together. Most of the sugar will dissolve in the mixture.

Step 3: Add the egg to the buttery mixture, beating it in well. More of the sugar will dissolve.

MIXING

Step 4: Add the flour and the cocoa to the mixture, and stir well. A thick, moist dough will form.

Step 5: Roll out the dough until it is about 5mm thick. Cut your cookies into shapes. Ensure that each cookie shape is the same size so they finish cooking at the same time.

PROTEIN CHANGING

Step 6: Place your cookie shapes onto an oven tray which has been lightly greased with some butter. Bake your cookies in a preheated oven at 190^0 C for 12–15 minutes.

CRYSTALLISATION

Step 7: The cookies may still be soft when you remove them from the oven. They will harden as they cool down.

WHAT HAPPENED?

The soft butter in the cookie mixture melted in the hot oven. The heat in the melted butter cooked the other ingredients. As the egg heated up, the proteins inside it tangled themselves up into a solid. After your cooked cookies cooled, the sugar also cooled and crystallised. This made the cookies hard and crunchy!

WHAT TO DO NOW?

After a busy time experimenting in a kitchen laboratory, protein pikelets and chemicookies make the most magnificent snacks. The best part about cooking is being able to eat the results!

5. Lovely Laboratory Loaf

Bread is probably one of the oldest foods that humans have learned to cook. The recipes for making some types of bread haven't changed much in 5,000 years! In this recipe, tiny living things will cause a chemical reaction in the mixture. Then, heat and moisture will turn the starch inside flour into something soft and delicious: the best fresh, white bread you've ever tasted!

LOVELY LABORATORY LOAF

Chemicals you will need:
- 3/4 cup of warm water.
- 1/4 teaspoon of sugar.
- $1^1/_2$ teaspoons of yeast.
- 4 cups of flour.
- 1 teaspoon of salt.
- Another 1 teaspoon of sugar.
- 2 tablespoons of oil.
- Another 3/4 cup of warm water.
- A little more oil.
- Another cup of flour to coat the flat surface.

Equipment you will need:
- A small bowl.
- A large bowl.
- A mixing spoon.
- A flat surface, like a bench.
- A pastry brush.
- Two loaf tins.

REMEMBER: Read the safety rules on page 6 carefully before you begin this recipe experiment!

DISSOLVING

Step 1: Put 3/4 cup of warm water and 1/4 teaspoon of sugar in the small bowl. Once the sugar has dissolved, sprinkle the yeast over the top of the liquid. Leave the covered bowl in a warm place for ten minutes.

The water and the sugar provide the yeast with food and drink. The yeast will only come alive in warm temperatures.

MIXING

Step 2: Mix 4 cups of flour, the salt, and the other 1 teaspoon of sugar together in the large bowl.

Yeast

Yeast is a tiny living organism. Even though it looks like a dried powder, it is really just waiting for something to eat and drink. Once it gets some food and drink in a warm temperature, it will come alive again! As it eats and drinks, it uses oxygen and produces carbon dioxide. The carbon dioxide gas forms the bubbles inside bread that creates a light and airy texture.

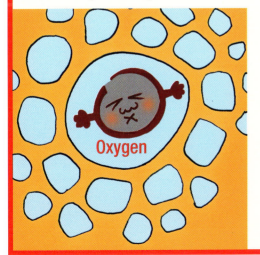
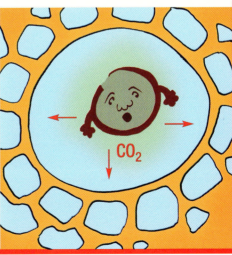

MIXING

Step 3: Into the large bowl, pour 2 tablespoons of oil, the other 3/4 cup of warm water, and the yeast mixture. Mix them all together to form a thick dough.

In the first ten minutes, the yeast was given enough food, water and warmth to wake up. Now, it finds itself in another warm place, surrounded by more delicious food.

Step 4: Knead the dough on a flat floured surface. Knead the dough by pushing it flat, folding it over, and pushing it flat again. Continue kneading for eight minutes. It's hard work!

Just like people, yeast needs plenty of air to breathe. When we knead the dough, we are squashing lots of tiny air bubbles into it.

Matzah

About 3,000 years ago, the Ancient Israelites were kept as slaves by the Egyptians. Jewish tradition says that when they decided to escape, they had no time to let their bread dough rise. They had to eat flat, unrisen bread instead. Today, at Passover, Jewish people celebrate their escape from Ancient Egypt by eating a special flat bread called matzah.

REACTING

Step 5: Now it's time to stop your work, and let the yeast do the work for you! Brush the large bowl with oil, before placing the ball of dough back in. Relax!

While you're relaxing, a chemical reaction takes place inside the yeast. It continues eating the sugar and drinking the water in the dough, and enjoying the warm temperature. As the yeast breathes, it produces another gas — carbon dioxide. Soon, there is so much carbon dioxide that the dough starts to fill with gas and rises until it doubles in size! This process usually takes about 30 minutes.

Step 6: To keep the yeast working hard, flatten the ball of dough, and knead it again for another five minutes.

Step 7: Divide and shape the dough into two loaf-shaped lumps. Place each lump of dough into loaf tins. After 30–45 minutes, the dough will have doubled in size again.

HEATING

Step 8: Place the loaf tins into a preheated oven at 200^0 C for 30 minutes. Enjoy the fabulous smell!

WHAT HAPPENED?

As the temperature increased inside the baked bread, the yeast died. But, the carbon dioxide bubbles from the yeast made the bread light and airy. The heat and moisture turned the starch inside the flour into large, soft clumps. As hydrogen and oxygen burned away in the hot oven, a lovely golden brown colour formed on the outside. With laboratory loaves as good as these, you won't need to buy white bread ever again!

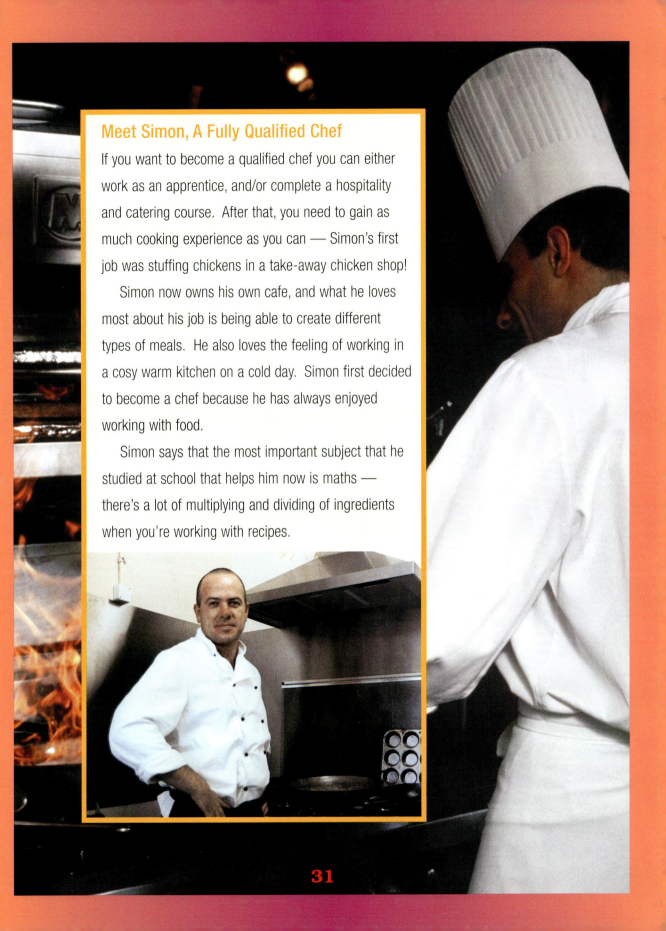

Meet Simon, A Fully Qualified Chef

If you want to become a qualified chef you can either work as an apprentice, and/or complete a hospitality and catering course. After that, you need to gain as much cooking experience as you can — Simon's first job was stuffing chickens in a take-away chicken shop!

Simon now owns his own cafe, and what he loves most about his job is being able to create different types of meals. He also loves the feeling of working in a cosy warm kitchen on a cold day. Simon first decided to become a chef because he has always enjoyed working with food.

Simon says that the most important subject that he studied at school that helps him now is maths — there's a lot of multiplying and dividing of ingredients when you're working with recipes.

Index

boiling points 8
carbon 9, 19, 22
carbon dioxide 11, 15, 22, 27, 29, 30
carbon monoxide 11
celsius 7
chef qualifications 31
chemical codes 9
chemicookies 23–25
crystallisation 10, 23, 25
diabetes 15
evaporation 12
hokey pokey 14–16
hydrogen 9, 12, 19, 22, 30
laboratory loaf 26–29
maths 31
matzah 28
molecules 8, 10, 13
onions 5
oxygen 9, 12, 19, 22, 27, 30
ovens 18
protein 13, 20, 21, 22, 24–25
protein pikelets 20–22
rice pudding 17–19
safety 6
starch 17, 26, 30
TV chefs 5
yeast 27

Bookweb Links

Read more Bookweb 6 books about food, nutrition and cooking:

Vitality — Factual
Vote For Us! — Factual
Autumn Moon — Fiction
No Way Home — Fiction

And here's a Bookweb 6 book about food we may eat in the future!

The Imaginer — Fiction

Key To Bookweb Fact Boxes
☐ Arts
☐ Health
☐ Science
☐ SOSE
☐ Technology